7/16 $21

JANE
ADDAMS

Social Worker and
Nobel Peace Prize Winner

Bonnie Carman Harvey

Enslow Publishers, Inc.
40 Industrial Road
Box 398
Berkeley Heights, NJ 07922
USA
http://www.enslow.com

Originally published as *Jane Addams: Nobel Prize Winner and Founder of Hull House* in 1999.

Library of Congress Cataloging-in-Publication Data

Harvey, Bonnie C.
 Jane Addams : social worker and Nobel Peace Prize winner / Bonnie Carman Harvey.
    pages cm. — (Lengedary American biographies)
 Includes bibliographical references and index.
    ISBN 978-0-7660-6461-4 (pbk.)— ISBN 978-0-7660-6460-7 — ISBN 978-0-7660-6462-1 (ebook) 1. Addams, Jane, 1860-1935—Juvenile literature. 2. Women social workers—United States—Biography—Juvenile literature. 3. Women social reformers—United States—Biography—Juvenile literature. 4. Hull House (Chicago, Ill.)—Juvenile literature. I. Title.
  HV40.32.A33H372 2015
  361.92—dc23
  [B]
                                   2014029286

Printed in the United States of America
102014 Bang Printing, Brainerd, Minn.
10 9 8 7 6 5 4 3 2 1

Future Editions:
Paperback ISBN: 978-0-7660-6461-4
EPUB ISBN: 978-0-7660-6462-1
Single-User PDF ISBN: 978-0-7660-6463-8
Multi-User PDF ISBN: 978-0-7660-6464-5

To Our Readers: We have done our best to make sure all Internet Addresses in this book were active and appropriate when we went to press. However, the author and the publisher have no control over and assume no liability for the material available on those Internet sites or on other Web sites they may link to. Any comments or suggestions can be sent by e-mail to comments@enslow.com or to the address on the back cover.

♻ Enslow Publishers, Inc., is committed to printing our books on recycled paper. The paper in every book contains 10% to 30% post-consumer waste (PCW). The cover board on the outside of each book contains 100% PCW. Our goal is to do our part to help young people and the environment too!

Illustration Credits: Library of Congress, p. 4;Shutterstock.com, © A-R-T (scrolls)

Cover Illustration: Library of Congress

CONTENTS

Jane Addams

Chapter 1

THE NOBEL PEACE PRIZE

As the distinguished crowd of scientists, literary figures, and humanitarians eagerly waited, the 1931 Nobel Prize ceremony in Stockholm, Sweden, was about to begin. In Oslo, Norway, a similar crowd had gathered for the awarding of the Nobel Peace Prize. Alfred Nobel, the founder of the Nobel Prizes, died on December 10, 1896. The annual ceremony commemorates the date of his death.

At the 1931 ceremony in Oslo, Miss Jane Addams was awarded the Nobel Peace Prize. She became the first American woman to receive a Nobel Prize. Then seventy-one, Addams was unable to attend the Nobel ceremonies because of illness. A Norwegian professor, Halvan Koht, spoke following the awarding of the Peace Prize, devoting much of his speech to Jane Addams's achievements. He noted,

> She is the foremost woman of her nation, not far from being its greatest citizen. . . . When the need was greatest she made the American woman's desire for peace an international interest. . . . In Jane Addams there are assembled all the best womanly attributes which shall help us to establish peace in the world. . . .[1]

Addams had been chosen for the Nobel Peace Prize with another American, Dr. Nicholas Murray Butler, president of Columbia University in New York. Like Addams, Butler had been involved in various peace movements. Addams resented Butler's being named a recipient, since he had strongly supported World War I and had denounced opponents of the war like Addams. The Nobel Committee, explaining why Jane Addams and Nicholas Butler were both chosen as the 1931 Peace Prize recipients, said the two had spent a lifetime "in trying to raise the ideal of peace in their people and in the whole world." The committee added, speaking of Jane Addams: "We also pay homage to the work which women can do for the cause of peace and fraternity among nations. For twenty-five years she has been the faithful spokesman of the idea of peace."[2]

Addams was at a friend's home, recovering from bronchitis, when she first learned of her award in November 1931. When her nephew, James Linn, came to see her, she teased him:

"I have something to tell you, but I'd better not. It is strictly confidential."

"About your operation?"

"Oh, that? No; that will come along presently. This is something nicer."

"What is it?" he asked.

"Go over to the bureau and open the second drawer on the left. There is a telegram on top of things. You can read it, but you must be quiet." Addams had been notified of her being awarded the Nobel Peace Prize. She was delighted.[3]

At the time of the Nobel Prize award ceremony, Jane Addams was very ill in a Baltimore, Maryland, hospital, awaiting surgery. Addams received the prize, which the American ambassador to Norway accepted for her, with characteristic humility. Because she was the first American woman to receive a Nobel Prize, Addams was honored.

Alfred Nobel

Alfred Nobel was born in Stockholm, Sweden, on October 21, 1833. Educated as a chemist, Nobel invented dynamite in 1866 by compounding nitroglycerin (made by mixing nitric acid and sulfuric acid with glycerol) with ammonium nitrate or cellulose nitrate. The countries of Sweden, Germany, and the United States began to manufacture dynamite almost at once. Nobel erected a plant at Ardeer, Scotland, in 1871, that became the largest dynamite factory in the world.

Within three months, when Addams was recovering from her surgery in Florida, her $16,000 share of the money from the Nobel Prize arrived. Addams wrote a letter to the Nobel Committee, explaining what she planned to do with the money. She told them:

> The award is to go to the International W.I.L.P.F. [Women's International League for Peace and Freedom], $12,000 invested as an endowment. . . . In case the W.I.L. ever comes to an end or is ever given up, I should like the money to revert to the international work of the Foreign Service Committee of the Society of Friends [the Quakers].[4]

Addams appreciated being the Nobel Peace Prize recipient more for the ways she could further the cause of world peace than for herself. She was showered with congratulatory messages from people everywhere.

The Nobel Prize was just one of many honors that came to Addams during the late 1920s and early 1930s. *Good Housekeeping* magazine named her "The first among twelve of the greatest living women in America."[5] Later in the year, Mark A. Dewolf Howe, a Boston writer and Pulitzer Prize winner, chose Addams as "one of the six most outstanding present-day Americans," the other five being men.[6]

Also in 1931, the alumnae of Bryn Mawr College in Pennsylvania awarded Addams the M. Carey Thomas Prize for her "great contribution to American living." Even former President Theodore Roosevelt said he considered Addams "the best argument for women's suffrage."[7]

Many other honors and awards were heaped upon this remarkable woman—largely because of her never ceasing efforts to reach out and assist poor people in the cities. Addams's goal was to be a neighbor to the poor people of Chicago—and the world.

Addams had decided early in her life that only through the elimination of all the poverty and ignorance she saw could she know victory over these terrible evils. Addams's goal was a monumental task for a rather small, plain-looking woman. But whatever she lacked in stature and strength, she made up for in strong will and determination.

Chapter 2

A COUNTRY CHILDHOOD

J ane Addams's happy childhood influenced her entire life. The small rural town of Cedarville, Illinois, where Jane grew up, was probably one of the best places for an impressionable girl to spend her childhood. Not only the influence of her family but also the opportunities provided by nature stimulated young Jane's imagination. From an early age, the sensitive girl reached out to those who were less fortunate.

Addams's Family

Jane's desire to help people—especially those who lived in poverty—came in part from her deeply religious ancestors. Her parents, John Huy Addams and Sarah Weber Addams, had moved to Illinois from Pennsylvania, where their ancestors had lived since colonial times. Robert Adams came from England in 1681 and received a land grant from William Penn; his brother Walter soon joined him in America. The brothers were some of the earliest Pennsylvanians. Evidently, Isaac, Walter's son and

Jane's great-grandfather, became the first "Addams" to add an extra d to avoid confusion with a relative by the same name. Isaac Addams's son, Samuel, became the father of John Huy Addams, Jane's father.

John Huy Addams, born in 1822, grew up in a fertile farming area near Pennsylvania Dutch country. He was a hardworking, God-fearing man influenced by his Quaker neighbors. As a young man, he became an apprentice to a flour mill owner, learning every facet of mill operation. Applying himself diligently, he developed self-discipline and industriousness, and a love of books and ideas. Later, Jane would become an eager admirer of her father's qualities and habits.[1]

John Addams fell in love with Sarah Weber, who was from another small town in Pennsylvania. Sarah had received a good education and was talented in music and art. She and John were married in 1844, and a short time later set out for the frontier state of Illinois. Several of Sarah's father's relatives had migrated to Illinois. They told the family back east of endless opportunities in the rapidly growing region. So John and Sarah made the decision to go west. They had a substantial sum of money, which John soon invested in his own sawmill and a gristmill on the banks of the Cedar River, near what would become the little community of Cedarville, Illinois. John searched for a long time for exactly the right place for his mill. Prior to finding a good location, he had entered in his diary, "I hope and pray God some permanent light may soon appear." He added that he and Sarah wanted to "settle down in life to do honor to God and selves."[2]

Jane Addams's Childhood

As the mill began to operate smoothly and John Addams became one of the leading citizens in the rural community, he built a substantial brick home for his family, overlooking Cedar Creek.

Pennsylvania Dutch

The descendants of German and Swiss immigrants who settled in Pennsylvania in the seventeenth and eighteenth centuries are called Pennsylvania Dutch. The dialect of High German spoken by these people and the style of folk art and decorative arts they developed are also called Pennsylvania Dutch. These settlers are characterized by their handwoven bedspreads in brilliant reds and blues, homespun linens, wonderful hospitality, and the enjoyment of bountiful meals.

John and Sarah Addams's children were all born there. Jane was the youngest, born on September 6, 1860—just months before the Civil War erupted in April 1861. When Jane was two years old, her mother died in childbirth (along with the newborn baby), leaving seventeen-year-old Mary to mother her four younger siblings: Martha, thirteen; Weber, ten; Alice, nine; and Jane (known as Jenny to her family). Mary ran the house with the aid of the Addamses' old nurse, Polly, and some outside helpers.

Her mother's death left an emptiness in Jane's life that caused her to become very devoted to her father. She wanted to be just like him. John Addams's integrity, honesty, and moral views opposing slavery greatly impressed Jane. Jane later remembered

> . . . "horrid nights" when I tossed about in my bed because I had told a lie. I was held in the grip of a miserable dread of death, a double fear, first, that I myself should die in my sins and go straight to that fiery Hell which was never mentioned at home . . . and, second, that my father . . . should himself die before I had time to tell him.[3]

These thoughts came to her, she recalled, from hearing the other children talk—and, most likely, from the Bible teaching in the village church.

Important Childhood Incidents

One of Jane's earliest memories was when, at three years old, she had burst into her father's study to find he had a visitor—a young black man. Since Illinois was a Northern, nonslaveholding state, not many blacks lived there. But the slave state of Kentucky, to the south of Illinois, had a large black population—many of whom were slaves. When her father signaled her to leave, Jane tiptoed quietly out the door.

Later, Jane's father spoke to her, urging her not to mention what she had seen to anyone. Only when she was much older did she learn that her father was involved in the Underground

Railroad, helping to hide escaped slaves on their way to freedom in Canada. People who participated in the Underground Railroad let fugitive slaves hide in their homes or other buildings, then found a way for them to travel to the next town. If caught, the fugitives faced terrible punishment, sometimes even death. The people who hid them had to pay large fines and could be sent to prison if they were discovered.

Anyone who reported a person involved in hiding slaves would be given a good sum of money by government officials because of the Fugitive Slave Law of 1850. The law made it a criminal offense to help runaway slaves. Any individual choosing to hide slaves took a great risk. He or she had to possess deep convictions and much courage. Because of the esteem John Addams enjoyed in his community—and because of his carefulness—no one ever reported him for his ties to the Underground Railroad.

Another of Jane's earliest memories was President Abraham Lincoln's death, which occurred when she was four and a half years old. She had noticed the two white gate posts in front of their house draped with American flags and bands of black cloth. Running into the house to learn the reason, she found her father in tears. Her father announced that the greatest man in the world had died, and Jane realized something terrible had happened.

She associated Abraham Lincoln with the dreadful war that had just ended. The Civil War had been fought between the Northern and Southern states largely over the issue of slavery. But the war also concerned the argument of individual states' rights as opposed to the federal government's rights. Young children like Jane could not fully understand what was taking place during the Civil War, but they knew it must be terrible when men fought and killed each other. Largely due to Abraham Lincoln's efforts, slavery was abolished as a result of the Civil War. Because of her father's high regard for President Lincoln, it

Abolition Movement

The abolition movement hoped to end slavery in the United States. Blacks as well as whites joined its ranks, and both women and men became active participants. Some of the best-known abolitionists included William Lloyd Garrison, who founded a newspaper called The Liberator to address the slavery issue; Wendell Phillips, Charles Sumner, and other outstanding orators; future suffragists like Lucretia Mott; as well as former slaves like Frederick Douglass, who became an influential writer and orator. The great achievement of the abolition movement was to make slavery an issue that could not be ignored.

was only natural that Jane, too, would think highly of him, even though she was just a child.

At the time of the war, there was an engraved plaque hanging on the living room wall, entitled "Addams's Guard."[4] When she wanted to see it closely, Jane would pull up a chair, place the family Bible and a dictionary on top, and stand on them to read the names of men who fought in the Civil War in the regiment called Addams's Guard. John Addams had served several terms as an Illinois state legislator and had known Abraham Lincoln personally. The Addams's Guard regiment was no doubt attached to John Addams's name as an honor for some service given to the president. The men whose names were on the "Addams's Guard" plaque were all from Jane's neighborhood. Whenever her family planned a drive, Jane would suggest a route past the home of one of the men of Addams's Guard.[5]

First Experience with Poverty

As an impressionable six-year-old, Jane caught her first glimpse of poverty. She had gone on a business trip with her father to a nearby mill town. In a poor section of the city, Jane asked her father why people lived in such "horrid little houses so close together." His explanation was that it was the only place they could afford to live.[6] Jane declared that when she was grown, she would have a large house next to the "horrid little houses" and live there. That way, the children in those houses could come and play in her yard—and maybe she could help them.

Childhood Insecurities

Jane admired her father intensely—perhaps because he was her only parent for a number of years after her mother's death. In her eyes, her father possessed unmatched wisdom and character. She was very proud of him. She also considered him very handsome in appearance and in the way he carried himself.

One Sunday, Jane walked beside her father to the village church, where he taught a Bible class. Jane had had a curved spine from birth, which caused her head to lean to one side. Painfully conscious of her slight deformity, she thought of herself as an "Ugly Duckling."[7] On this Sunday, some strangers had visited the church, and Jane, believing her handsome father would not want to be seen with an "ugly duckling," began to walk home with her uncle James. Her uncle took her hand, saying, "So you are going to walk with me to-day?"[8] Neither her father nor her uncle ever suspected Jane's real motive in choosing to walk with her uncle.

The various experiences Jane had during her childhood influenced her greatly. At the age of six, she dreamed night after night that

> every one in the world was dead excepting myself, and that upon me rested the responsibility of making a wagon wheel. . . . The next morning would often find me . . . standing in the doorway of the village blacksmith shop, anxiously watching the [blacksmith] at work. I would store my mind with such details of the process . . . as I could observe . . . [then] sigh heavily and walk away, bearing my responsibility as best I could, and this of course I confided to no one.[9]

This dream, along with her first look at poverty, seems to have made Jane believe that she was the only one who could do something about poverty—just like in her dream, she was the only one who could make the first wagon wheel.

A New Stepfamily

When Jane was seven, her father married Anna Haldeman, a widow with two sons. George, who was six months younger than Jane, became her constant playmate. Together they explored the

Old Abe

An eagle had been carried as a mascot by the 8th Wisconsin Regiment of the Union forces throughout the Civil War. It was nicknamed Old Abe after President Abraham Lincoln and was kept at the state capitol of Wisconsin, where the bird was an honored war pensioner. Like the returning soldiers, Old Abe received a regular allowance that kept him supplied with food and necessities!

surrounding countryside. They played hide-and-seek in the dusty corners of her father's mill, and jumped and romped in the piles of grain.

Fascinated by the sawmill, Jane and George played a dangerous game. They would ride the logs moving into place and jump off just before they reached the grinding saw. Fortunately, they were never hurt playing this risky game! The two playmates also enjoyed the wide-open fields surrounding the house and the mill. They never tired of discovering secret hiding places and finding daring adventures to challenge them. These wonderful carefree days of her childhood gave Jane Addams the desire to help every child have the same kind of opportunities that she had had.

Jane learned many things from her father during her childhood. She learned to be practical. She also gained understanding in spiritual matters through her many long talks with her father. Above all, the little girl learned to be patient— just like her father. Jane usually attended the Bible class her father taught, where he talked about living a Christian life. John Addams considered himself a "Hicksite Quaker," or a person who followed the teachings of Elias Hicks. In addition to believing in the Bible, Hicks taught that a person should follow an "inner light" for guidance. He believed the inner light was God's voice speaking from within a person. Because of what her father believed, he trusted in God and his own convictions. He told Jane, "You must always be honest with yourself inside, whatever happens."[10] Jane thought her father's advice about truth and morality was as important as teachings from the Bible.

Jane also learned the need to help others, and the challenge that reaching out could be, from her father. One Sunday, Jane wore a new coat, which she could hardly wait to show to her fellow Bible class members. Her father frowned, telling her that he admired the coat, but she should not wear it to class, because most of the other children could not afford pretty new coats like hers. Dutifully, Jane removed her coat, put on her old one, and walked beside her father to church. She asked her father, "Why don't the other children have good new cloaks like mine?" Her father explained that some families do not have enough money for things they need and want. Jane responded, "Then what can be done about it?"[11] Her father failed to give her an answer. She spent the rest of her life seeking one.

Chapter 3

THE WORLD BEYOND CEDARVILLE

From the time she was nine until she turned seventeen in 1877, Jane Addams and her stepbrother George attended the little village school in Cedarville. Like most elementary schools in those days, the school was ungraded. Children of all ages gathered in one classroom and were taught by one teacher.

Many Books

Encouraged by her father, Jane had already read several difficult but well-known works, including translations of Homer and Virgil. However, she preferred historical books like *Plutarch's Lives* and Washington Irving's *Life of Washington*. Her father offered her small amounts of money for each book she read—but Jane got the money only after he "cross-examined" her about each book![1] Jane was expected to give a review of each book and answer any questions her father chose to ask.

At the village school, Jane excelled in Latin and English while George enjoyed biology and studying nature. George liked to collect bugs, butterflies, birds' eggs, snakes, worms, and cocoons. George's delight in science prompted a similar interest in Jane, and she began thinking of a career in medicine. For Jane even to think of a career was unusual at that time. Young girls were expected to stay at home, get married, and raise children. Jane Addams was different.

School Days

Even before she reached age seventeen, Jane had decided she wanted to go to college and get a degree. Her desire to attend college was extraordinary in those days when higher education was considered unnecessary for women. Jane's father was not happy about her decision. John Addams intended for his daughter to go to Rockford Female Seminary in Rockford, Illinois. Rockford Seminary simply gave young women an education beyond the elementary level—it was not a college. Jane's two sisters, Alice and Mary, had gone to Rockford. Besides, John Addams was a trustee of Rockford Seminary and felt he would lose face if his daughter went somewhere else.

Jane had her heart set on a college degree. In fact, she had already decided to attend Smith College in Northampton, Massachusetts. Of course, Mr. Addams could not understand why Jane wanted to go so far from home. He thought the matter would soon be resolved; that is, he thought Jane would simply put such foolish ideas out of her mind and attend Rockford Seminary. Mr. Addams wanted Jane to get an education—but only in preparation for getting married. He certainly did not think in terms of a career for her and could not have imagined the underlying ambition that motivated his daughter.

Mrs. Addams sided with Jane, hoping her stepdaughter would be able to attend to Smith College. She wanted Jane and her son George to marry at some point—and if Jane had a college degree from a prestigious eastern college, it would give Mrs. Addams more social prominence.

For months, Jane studied many hours each day in order to take the difficult entrance exams for Smith College. The exams were oral and were given only at Northampton. While she studied, she worried because her father still had not given his approval. Reluctantly, her father let her go east for the exam. He reasoned that she would probably fail the exams, and that would end her obsession with Smith College.

In the early spring of 1877, Jane traveled to Massachusetts to take the exams. By July she learned that she had been accepted to Smith. Jane's excitement could scarcely be contained. Her father's reaction, however, was mixed. Of course, he was proud of her, but he sensed he would have to resign his trusteeship at Rockford Seminary if his own daughter went elsewhere. Mr. Addams also wanted to keep Jane close to home. Thus, Mr. Addams told Jane his decision: "I have thought it over, Jane," he told her, "and you are to go to Rockford in the fall."[2]

Because of love and respect for her father, Jane complied with his wishes, although she was extremely disappointed. Within a few days, she received the Rockford Seminary brochure and studied it thoroughly.

Rockford Female Seminary

Jane was amazed that Rockford Seminary required her to take new entrance exams! Mr. Addams stated matter-of-factly, "Naturally. You could not expect us to accept the verdict of others. You will take them when you arrive in the fall."[3]

After taking in the news about further entrance exams, Jane made up a rigorous study schedule for herself and began to prepare. She would be questioned in eight subjects, and she was determined to make sure the results would be positive. Luckily, she had recently studied for the Smith College exams, so the subject matter was fresh in her mind.

In time, Jane's acceptance to Rockford came, and she prepared for the fall term. The college bulletin stated flatly that students were not to bring any jewelry. Because a number of the young ladies were expected to become missionaries, they would probably not need such worldly items as jewelry. Required items included a "knife, fork, and teaspoon; napkins, bed linen and blankets; towels and a year's supply of plain, inexpensive clothing, especially flannels. One pair of India Rubber overshoes, a waterproof cloak and an umbrella" completed the required list.[4]

Mr. Addams responded to Jane's look of astonishment at these last items, telling her that the principal, Anna Sill, "insists that the students walk an hour each day, rain or shine. She finds that such exercise improves the health."[5]

Jane enjoyed her new life at Rockford almost from the start. Finally, she had numerous people her own age with whom to form friendships. She even appreciated the care of the stern-looking Anna Sill, who presided over the two hundred students with an army sergeant's authority and rigor. Sill diligently watched over each girl's religion, health, and education. And yes, Sill held to the hour's daily walk for each girl—rain or shine.[6]

Classmates and College Life

One of the girls Jane liked best was Ellen Gates Starr, a fellow student. Before long, Jane and Ellen became close friends, spending many hours in deep discussion on various topics, but especially the topic of religion. (Little did they know that their friendship would last a lifetime.) They were well aware that Anna Sill had hopes that many of the girls would choose to work as missionaries.

However, Jane objected to the overused topic of "soul saving." She told Ellen,

> I read my Bible every day as you do, [and] I find that Jesus said there are two commandments. He says we should love God—and I do. But He says, too, "Love thy neighbor as thyself." Perhaps my neighbor is as important as my own soul—yet I hear little about that second commandment.[7]

Jane rejected the idea of emphasizing Bible teaching over simply aiding people in whatever ways they needed help.

Despite Ellen's frequent disagreements with Jane's point of view, Jane refused to change her beliefs. Ellen sided with Sill—believing their duty was to convert non-Christians by becoming missionaries—but she and Jane remained good friends despite their differences. Ellen began teaching and did not return to Rockford; however, the two friends stayed in touch through letters.

The course of study Jane followed was a common one at the time: Latin, Greek, French, history, literature, and Jane's favorite: Mental and Moral Philosophy. Rockford did not offer a college degree at that time. Provisions for additional courses to fulfill college requirements, however, were already in Rockford's charter. The idea of a college degree became an obsession with Jane and another friend, Catherine "Kitty" Waugh. Both young women registered for courses in higher mathematics and increased their Latin and Greek studies in order to qualify for college degrees.[8]

Speaker and Debater

After studying hard all week, weekends were relatively free. Jane always looked forward to weekends—either to go buggy or sleigh riding with George, to travel to Cedarville or another familiar place, or simply to relax. Early on Sunday mornings, she and her favorite teacher, Mary Blaisdell, would read the New

Testament in the original Greek language and discuss the spiritual implications of the text. Jane savored this time.[9]

Jane began to excel in her studies during her second year at Rockford. She was often at the head of her classes. After classroom hours her room always filled with friends discussing issues of the day, such as Charles Darwin's theory of evolution, the latest scientific ideas, and literary works by Victorian writers like Thomas Carlyle. Although Rockford Seminary did not have a formal debating club, these sessions in Jane's room sharpened her speaking skills, and she emerged a good debater. Soon she was chosen to compete in the Interstate Oratorical Contest in Jacksonville, Illinois. The importance of this contest lay not only in the honor for Rockford Seminary but also in the rare opportunity for women to compete.[10]

The competition in the contest proved to be intense. One of the debaters was William Jennings Bryan, a young college student from Illinois College. In later years, he would win fame as an orator and politician. Though he did not win first place, Bryan placed higher than Jane, who finished somewhere in the middle. When Jane returned to her campus, a great celebration awaited her. The mood turned sour as her friends and classmates discovered she had not won the competition. Nearly everyone in the school had listened to and critiqued Jane's speeches before she left and had thought she would automatically win. Many of the students were angry with Jane for not winning!

Jane soon became occupied with other activities and dismissed the ill-fated contest. She wrote articles for the *Rockford Seminary* magazine, which she edited during her senior year. Her writing tended to be thoughtful and somewhat weighty. At graduation time, Jane received honors and was selected to give the valedictory address. In her address, Jane paid tribute to Anna Sill for the fine work she had done in overseeing her young charges. Despite Sill's failure to persuade Jane to become a

William Jennings Bryan (1860-1925)

Called the "Great Commoner" or the "Boy Orator of the Platte," Bryan was an American lawyer and politician who campaigned unsuccessfully for the presidency in 1896, 1900, and 1908. He became famous for his fierce "Cross of Gold" speech advocating free silver (1896) and for his defense of fundamentalism in the Scopes "Monkey" trial (1925).

missionary, Jane admired her immensely. Jane received only a certificate of graduation, but she had completed the necessary courses for a college degree, which would be given to her the following year at graduation. Rockford Seminary needed to make certain changes to qualify the institution as a college.

After graduation, Jane would be off to new fields of endeavor. She had decided to become a doctor and to help the poor. However these two desires could be woven together, Jane resolved to do it.[11]

Chapter 4

A CHANGE OF DIRECTION

Graduation ended, and Jane Addams piled her books into her father's buggy for the trip back to Cedarville. As she thought about the graduation ceremony, she thrilled once more to recall Anna Sill's words that she, Jane Addams, had attained a college degree—to be awarded at commencement in 1882—the following year. Kitty Waugh, too, had qualified. All their hard work and effort had paid off.

Unexpected Death

Now that she had time to think about the future, she was confused. What would she do now? Among the items she unpacked once she reached home was a copy of a *Rockford Seminary* magazine that contained an article she had written earlier that year. Addams went back over her words:

> Always do what you are afraid to do! Once I believed that. Now I know that to do what you are afraid to do is to have your life guided by fear. How much better not to be afraid to do what you believe in doing! Keep one main idea, and you will never be lost.[1]

The person who wrote those words seemed so sure of herself! But now the Jane Addams who had composed those words had no idea what to do next.

She envied the girls who had no doubts about their life's course after graduation. They were either going to become missionaries, teach, or get married. The girls had few choices—but at least they knew what they were going to do. Almost in a panic, Addams sent her records and application to the Woman's Medical College of Philadelphia. Before long, she received word of her acceptance in the fall of 1881 as a beginning medical student. Once more, Addams proved to be a pioneer, because the field of medicine had just begun to open up to women. The Woman's Medical College of Philadelphia was the first college in the world organized to provide a medical education for women.

The summer turned out to be a pleasant one. George had returned from college. He had also graduated and planned to attend Johns Hopkins Medical School in the fall. And as usual, Mrs. Addams held a series of parties and invited numerous young people to join the festivities.

When her father suggested that Jane and George accompany him and Mrs. Addams on a trip to northern Michigan, Jane Addams joyfully accepted. When she returned home from Rockford, she had become quite depressed as she agonized over what to do with her life. Then, the spinal curvature problem she had suffered since her childhood began to plague her, and her family convinced her that she would not be able to go to medical school. The trip her father proposed would give Jane time to think and to make new plans.

However, as they traveled along, enjoying the warm August sun, Mr. Addams suddenly became ill with acute appendicitis. With great alarm, the family took him to Green Bay, Wisconsin, where he died several hours later. Returning home, the family had John Addams buried in the family cemetery plot next to Jane's mother.

After the funeral, as Jane Addams trudged over the narrow bridge spanning the little backyard creek, she suddenly felt very alone. All her life she had looked to her father for guidance and approval, and now he was gone. For three or four weeks, her life stood still. She was aimless. Everyone else in the household had something to do: Mary was married, George was about to enter Johns Hopkins Medical School, and Mrs. Addams wanted to close up the house and move to a larger city.

Medical School

Then one September day as Jane came into the dining room, she heard George and his mother discussing railroad tickets. George would be leaving the following Monday for medical school in Maryland. Earlier, her family had told her that her health would not allow her to go to medical school, so she had decided against it. Suddenly, she remembered that her medical school acceptance was still available.

"But I was going East, too!" she cried. "You can't leave me here, George!"[2]

Even though George seemed pleased at the idea of having her company, his mother was not sure Addams was up to the trip so soon after her father's death.

However, Addams reassured her: "I shall be better. I shall stop sitting around feeling sorry for myself. I shall go when George does—you'll help me, won't you?"[3]

Before long, Addams was packed and ready to go. Due to John Addams's death, Mrs. Addams decided to close the Cedarville house and travel to Philadelphia with Addams. There, she would be near George in Baltimore.

Once Addams was settled in medical school, she worked very hard, excelling in her studies. From the fall of 1881 to the spring of 1882, she studied countless hours and tried to forget the pain of her father's death. She passed her examinations, but at the same time, her health began to fail. She experienced terrible pain in her back from her spinal curvature and was hospitalized for some time.

Addams's health improved enough for her to go home to Cedarville, although she was still in great pain. She managed to make the trip to Rockford Seminary in June 1882 to receive her coveted college degree. When she came back to Cedarville, she left almost at once to visit her sister Alice and Alice's husband, Dr. Harry Haldeman (Addams's stepbrother), in Mitchellville, Iowa. Dr. Haldeman believed Addams's curvature of the spine could be corrected with surgery.

Dr. Haldeman performed the delicate surgery, which was successful. However, Addams did have to remain stretched out on a board for six months, and then she had to use a heavy steel and whalebone brace that covered her entire midsection and acted as a crutch under her arms. She still experienced much pain but bore it as bravely as she could.[4] Because of the surgery, Addams found it necessary to withdraw from medical school.

Trip Abroad

At this point, Mrs. Addams came to Jane Addams's rescue by suggesting a trip to Europe. In 1883, Mrs. Addams, Jane, and six others, including some cousins, sailed aboard the *Servia*. In the late 1800s, all educated Americans wanted to make what was called the "Grand Tour"—that is, some kind of journey in which they paid homage to their roots and ancestral ties. At that time, Europeans were considered culturally superior to Americans. To acquire polish, a refined American was expected to make this European journey.[5]

Like a typical tourist, Addams kept a journal of her trip. One of her entries noted that famous Americans like novelist Henry James were aboard the ship. Another entry, written when they were in Ireland, mentioned a number of interesting sights, including Blarney Castle, which contains the Blarney stone. Following their tour of Ireland, the party spent time traveling in Scotland, then went on to the English Lake District, home of the poets William Wordsworth and Samuel Taylor Coleridge, and finally, on to London.

Mile End Road

Since they planned to spend a good deal of time in London, the party found a comfortable place to stay and began to sightsee in various parts of the city. On a Saturday evening shortly after their arrival, the group went on a tour of London conducted by a city guide. They were taken to Mile End Road, where they could watch the Saturday night sale of decaying fruits and vegetables. The produce had to be sold that night because of Sunday laws that prohibited buying and selling. Addams wrote in her journal about the poorly dressed, starving people gathered around two "hucksters' carts":

> They were bidding . . . for a vegetable held up by the auctioneer, which he at last scornfully flung, with a gibe for its cheapness, to the successful bidder. . . . one man detached himself from the group. He had bidden [on] a cabbage, and when it struck his hand, he instantly sat down on the curb, tore it with his teeth, and hastily devoured it, unwashed and uncooked as it was.[6]

This scene of ragged, filthy people reaching out for rotten produce made an impression on Jane Addams that she would never forget. The indifference of the omnibus driver shocked Addams as he boasted, "What'd I tell you, lady? A sight, isn't it?"[7]

Addams did not answer. She could not. She wanted to help those poor people. But what could she do? She was just one small woman, still wearing a brace from her recent surgery. Maybe she could not do much—but she would find a way to do something.

Chapter 5

LIFE'S WORK AT LAST

Questions raced through Addams's mind. Where would she begin? How would she put her ideas into practice? She was not sure how to proceed, but at least now she had a clearer idea about something she could do. She had to find a way to help people like those she had just seen at Mile End Road—and the ones she had seen in the mill town near Cedarville as a little girl.

Out-of-the-Way Sightseeing

Before his death, her father had planned for his daughter to spend two years touring Europe. This length of time for travel was quite typical for wealthy Americans of the day. A trip to Europe in the 1800s involved much more time and effort than it does today. The ocean voyage alone took several weeks. Thankful for the ample time to think and plan, Addams continued the tour with her stepmother and the others in their group.

Now that she had decided what she should do for her life's work, Addams took advantage of her stay in London. She stole away at every opportunity to visit poor sections of the city. Her stepmother had no idea she was doing such things and no doubt would have been quite upset. Mrs. Addams viewed these ideas of her stepdaughter's as "philanthropic nonsense."[1]

These were difficult days for Addams. Both her stepmother and George opposed her ideas of reaching out to poor people. They considered such behavior inappropriate for someone in Addams's social situation. The entire concept of social work and helping unfortunate people barely existed at that time. Mrs. Addams harassed her stepdaughter about marrying George and settling down. Mrs. Addams herself relished mixing with well-to-do people and attending parties, lectures, and other social gatherings. She thought Addams should like them, too. But Addams was miserable in those surroundings. Her greatest happiness came from visiting the poor sections of a city and thinking of ways the people's lives could be improved.

She wondered whether anyone else cared about these wretched people and wanted to help them. Although Addams did not know it at the time, there was a group of Oxford University students who had banded together to aid the poor. One member of this group, Arnold Toynbee, tried some innovative experiments. Toynbee was trying to find ways to bridge the gap between rich and poor people. He had given some public talks on art in a poor section of the city and then told the people they could see some of his paintings. He wanted to enrich their lives. Later, he realized that to reach out to people living in poverty, he needed to live among them. He could also learn more about the causes and cure for poverty. He wanted to understand all about the poorer, working-class people, to learn about their problems and concerns. His ideas would later influence Addams greatly.

Addams continued with her stepmother and the others for the rest of the European tour. They visited Holland, Germany, Austria, Italy, Greece, and France. Addams enjoyed studying the languages of different countries. She also visited churches, art galleries, and museums. But closest to her heart were her visits to the slums of each city. There, she identified with the people and longed to do something to improve their lives. After twenty-one months, the tour came to an end, and the party left for America.

Although it was good to be back in Cedarville, Addams now sensed a restlessness within herself. She could not feel content anywhere for very long.

The correspondence between Addams and her good friend, Ellen Starr, began to increase. Addams poured out her heart to her friend, telling Starr of her dreams and desires to do something for poor people. Starr suggested that Addams reach out to the poor in Cedarville and in Freeport—both small Illinois towns. She tried. But the poor in those places at least enjoyed sunshine and had little gardens behind their cottages, unlike the poor in London's East End, who had absolutely nothing.

Because of the Industrial Revolution in both England and the United States, the gap between rich people and poor people had widened considerably. The Industrial Revolution was brought about by the increased use of machines and manufacturing to produce goods in the cities. In earlier years, many products were made in people's homes. Now, people were forced to move to crowded cities and work for low wages in factories. All these changes caused much upheaval in lower-class people's lives, resulting in untold misery. In the mid- to late-1800s, there were mainly two classes of people in both England and the United States: the rich and the poor.

Struggles to Find a Solution

After being home just a short time, Addams again found herself without a purpose. She had earlier decided against returning to medical school. Her heart was simply not in her studies. She did want to help the poor, but she did not need to be a doctor to do that. Since Addams and her sister Mary had always been close, she spent much time with Mary and her family. Through Mary's encouragement, Addams even joined the Presbyterian Church in Cedarville, where Mary's husband served as minister. Addams had never been a church member, but she held to Quaker teachings, like her father.

Fortunately, Addams's father had left her a sizable fortune for that day, so she had no need to concern herself with earning a living. Addams had inherited a 247-acre farm, sixty acres of timberland, and eighty acres of land in the Dakota Territory—as well as stock, bonds, and other property amounting to around $50,000 to $60,000.

From 1885 to 1887, Jane and Mrs. Addams spent their summers in Cedarville and their winters in Baltimore, Maryland, where George was attending medical school. Mrs. Addams enjoyed Baltimore's social life with its numerous parties, teas, and other events. Of course, Jane Addams was expected to attend these functions as well. Her stepmother also wished that Addams and George would marry, but that was out of the question for Jane. She simply did not love George—or anyone else for that matter—in a romantic way.

Addams soon wearied of the endless parties. She found herself becoming more interested in discovering Baltimore's charities than in meeting its fashionable people. Her interests lay more in visiting orphanages and shelters than in attending teas and parties—she never tired of being with the poor.

These visits made her do some serious thinking. There must be other women like herself with enough money and spare time but no real purpose in life. She knew, too, that many people could only dream of a life like hers. So many people were caught in jobs that paid next-to-nothing wages and lived in run-down neighborhoods. They could scarcely manage food and shelter, let alone think of spare time.[2] They were locked into their jobs and often worked under dreadful conditions in stuffy, cramped quarters that were hot in the summer and cold in the winter. Their homes were little better. Addams found herself unable to enjoy her wealth, knowing the terrible living conditions of so many other people.

Increasingly, her ideas began to take shape. Perhaps a way could be found to bring people—the rich and the poor— together so they could benefit each other. Surely the things the groups had in common would outweigh their numerous differences.

Another Beginning

As she thought about these ideas, she realized she needed time to think them over. In 1887, over two years after her trip abroad, Addams and a college friend decided to join Ellen Starr, who was traveling in Europe. Addams had decided to study early Christianity in Rome. Maybe she would find her purpose through additional study.

She arrived in England a few days before Christmas, 1887. At twenty-seven, she possessed a confidence she had lacked earlier as she studied art and languages and enjoyed sightseeing in the various countries. In Rome, some shocking news came: Her sister Mary's daughter, a little girl Addams loved very much, had died. While grief-stricken, Addams's old back pain flared up, and she had to stay in bed for a month while her friends continued traveling. When she felt well enough, she rejoined her friends in Spain.

On Easter, 1888, Addams and her friends were in Madrid, watching a bullfight. Because she had never seen a bullfight before, she found herself fascinated as the men on horseback taunted the bull with their long spears. The extreme cruelty

Bullfighting

The national sport in Spain, bullfighting is also popular in some regions of southern France and in some Latin American countries. Known as the corrida de toros (Spanish for "running of the bulls"), it is regarded as an art in Spain. Leading bullfighters, called matadors, are treated as national heroes. Picadors (horsemen who prod the bull with a lance to exhaust its neck and shoulder muscles) are sent into the bullring to weaken the bull before the matador enters the arena to make the final kill.

shocked her friends, and they left early, but Addams stayed. The angry bull killed the riders' horses; then, the men killed the bull. She watched the entire spectacle, barely moving. She was "entranced by the 'glories of the amphitheater.'"[3] She had been caught up in the bravery of the bullfighters, oblivious to the five bulls they had killed. When she finally left and caught up with her friends, they scolded her indifference to the cruelty to the helpless animals. Suddenly, she felt tried and condemned for delighting in the violence and for spending time watching it.

That evening, however, Addams was shocked at her earlier state of mind. She realized that she had remained idle herself, while making self-righteous charges against others. She had made some vague future idea of reform a reason for continuing with study and travel. As she suddenly realized, "I had fallen into the meanest type of self-deception in making myself believe that all this was in preparation for great things to come."[4]

Addams had made up her mind. From now on, she would act. She was done with simply talking about doing something to help the poor. The following morning she shared with Ellen Starr something that had been taking shape in her mind. The plan had begun when she visited Ulm Cathedral in Germany. There, she had observed that "All mankind seemed welcome and at home in Ulm Cathedral."[5] Observing the togetherness of all peoples, Addams thought of Ulm as a "'cathedral of humanity' dedicated to brotherhood, understanding, unity, and spiritual aspiration."[6] Surely she could build a modern "cathedral of humanity."

She proposed to Ellen Starr the possibility of renting a house in a city where the people had many extreme needs. There, they could reach out to people, touch their lives, and lift them up. Finally, they could have a house where they could put all the wonderful ideas they had learned in books and lectures into practice. Some of these ideas, teaching the brotherhood of mankind, were included in the works of Ralph Waldo Emerson,

Thomas Carlyle, John Ruskin, and others—all leading Victorian thinkers and writers. To Addams's amazement, Starr understood exactly what she meant. Even more astonishing, Starr promised to join her in putting her plan into effect.

After years of studying and searching for ways to help eliminate poverty, Jane Addams's goals had assumed a definite form. At last, she had found the means of putting her words and ideas into practice.

Chapter 6

FINDING THE RIGHT PLACE

Addams was excited about putting her ideas into action. But she knew she had a considerable amount of work ahead of her. Hearing about a missionary conference in London, she decided to go there while Ellen Starr remained in Paris. There was much Addams could learn from people who had lived in foreign countries, helping others. They could probably give her some suggestions about how she could help city people.

Visiting Toynbee Hall

Toynbee Hall turned out to be the highlight of Addams's London visit. Known as a settlement house, Toynbee Hall was a place where fifteen well-to-do young men, all university graduates, lived and worked among the poor. They referred to themselves as settlement workers since they "settled," or established their homes, in the middle of the poor community where they worked. These young men would do whatever they could to help the poor in their homes or in their work. They also expected to learn from the poor.

Another fascinating place Addams visited in London was the People's Palace, supported by gifts from wealthy people. The Palace was a neighborhood center in a poor section of London. It contained a swimming pool, a gymnasium, a library, and meeting rooms. It had been built in an extremely poor section of London for poor people to enjoy.

Impressed by Toynbee Hall and the People's Palace, Addams's ideas became more definite. She thought of starting a center like Toynbee Hall in the United States. Maybe she and Starr could enrich their neighbors' lives by adding touches of beauty. She thought of the many photographs and art prints they had gathered in their European travels. They could show these to their new neighbors. As an elementary school teacher, Starr could hold classes for the people. But Addams wondered what part she would play in this new venture. She would find her own part before long.

City Venture

Back in the United States, Addams and Starr had agreed to meet in Chicago in January 1889. Since Starr had taught at the Kirkland School in Chicago and knew a number of prominent people, the two friends decided to put their plans to work in that city. They had intended to come earlier, when the weather would be more cooperative, but personal plans intervened. Even though Addams's family tried to talk her out of her silly notions for a big house in a poor section of the city, she refused to listen to them. Now, as she and Starr rode in a carriage down Chicago's bustling streets, the softly falling snow made visibility difficult.

Chicago in 1889 was a bustling city. People from all over the world arrived daily to seek their fortunes. In fact, the population of over a million prided itself on being made up of immigrants. Italians, Germans, Irish, Poles, Scandinavians, Austrians,

Russians, and people from many other lands had come to Chicago, the "Gateway to Opportunity."[1]

Many of Chicago's newcomers did not speak English, so they wanted to live in communities with other immigrants from the same country. The result was that entire sections became like small foreign cities within the city. Many of these foreign sections had their own shops, newspapers, and churches in which their native language was spoken.

As Addams looked for the right house in Chicago, she visited several of these areas. Since she did not know much about Chicago, she asked newspapermen, real estate agents, and others to help her find a place.

Soon, her interest was drawn to Halsted Street, which, at about thirty-two miles long, was said to be the longest straight street in the world. Addams realized that several foreign neighborhoods were located around Halsted Street. The area was home to numerous Italians, Poles, Russians, Irish, and others who were very poor. Within a short distance after leaving these neighborhoods, one came to Ashland Avenue, a street where many well-to-do Chicagoans lived. Chicago was indeed a strange mixture of all types of people living close together.

Addams and Ellen Starr had rented a place near Halsted Street from which they could continue their search. Starr soon found a teaching position in a fine school on Chicago's north side, off Lake Michigan. When Starr's school day ended, the two friends would set out in a carriage to continue their search for just the right house. As they searched, they became better acquainted with Chicago. They drove down narrow, garbage-laden streets and alleys and saw the crowded tenements overflowing with people.

Most of the people living in the tenements worked long hours in factories or other places where they earned pitifully small wages. Before coming to America, many of these same

Chicago

Chicago is the third largest city in the United States. The first settlers arrived in the 1830s, and Chicago was on its way to becoming a city by 1837. Chicago developed as a result of its strategic position linking the Great Lakes with the Mississippi River. In 1871, much of the city was destroyed by fire but was quickly rebuilt. Today the city is the major industrial, commercial, financial, and cultural center for the Midwest. Known as the transportation center of the United States, Chicago has one of the nation's busiest airports. The city is also home to seven universities, the Sears Tower (one of the world's tallest buildings), and several professional sports teams.

people had gathered oranges in Spain or olives in Greece. Women who had gleaned wheat in the poppy-bright fields of Europe or dug peat in the bogs of Ireland now worked long hours in dismal factories.[2] Perhaps the wages earned in their own countries had been small, but at least they had enjoyed better working conditions near their homes.

Often, the faces of the people Addams saw in Chicago, with their weariness and their hopeless-looking eyes, reminded her of the people she had seen at London's Mile End Road and in other slum areas in Europe. But she also detected another kind of hunger in them—a hunger to see beautiful things and to experience some of life's joys.

The Right House

The house Addams chose had to be in the midst of as many immigrants as possible. It needed to be fairly large, too, and solidly built. She and Starr had searched for several months and seen hundreds of smaller houses that had been hastily built to accommodate Chicago's ever-increasing housing needs. Months had passed when, one Sunday afternoon, Addams mentioned to Starr that she thought she had seen just the right place. Earlier that day, Addams had seen a large brick house with white pillars and porches. The only problem was that she could not remember exactly where she had seen it!

Three weeks later, as she rode down Halsted Street, Addams spotted the same house. Excitedly, she cried out for the driver to stop in front of the magnificent brick house tightly wedged in between a saloon and a funeral home. This time she learned all she could about the house. Businessman Charles Hull had built the house thirty-three years earlier in the open countryside. The house had then fallen on hard times as the city grew around it. The first floor now held offices and warehouses, and a factory had been built just behind the house. Addams overlooked the

Settlement House

A settlement house provides community services in an underprivileged area. Often, the house offers classes and other types of assistance, but most of all, it reaches out in friendship to the people of the community. The educated people who live in and run the settlement house are much like the early pioneers in the United States. The very different living conditions are as new to them as the wilderness areas were to the original settlers.

grime and disarray of this once-beautiful mansion. As she stood looking at the house, Addams realized this was exactly what she had been looking for! Once Addams made arrangements to move into the house, she and Starr could put their plans of reaching out to the neighborhood poor into action.

Addams arranged to rent the second floor and a large room on the first floor. After moving in, Addams and Starr began the task of refurbishing and decorating the gracious old rooms. They brought in many of the beautiful pictures and photographs they had collected during their European travels. And Addams carefully picked out certain good pieces of her family's mahogany furniture and even put her parents' silver on display. She was determined to make her first home beautiful—no matter what other use would be made of the house.

Hull House Opens for Visitors

At long last, all was ready at Hull House—a name Addams and Starr quickly decided on, which gave credit to its original owner. The elegant, high-ceilinged rooms had been cleaned and painted, the furniture put in the right places, and each picture hung in the appropriate spot.

Even before Addams and Starr moved into Hull House, word had begun to spread about Addams's ideas of helping the poor. Magazines and newspapers published articles about her plans. People in the United States knew little at the time about settlement houses like London's Toynbee Hall. The idea of such houses was still quite new. Settlement houses were not charities or missions, but more like homesteads in the midst of slums.

On September 18, 1889, Addams and Starr moved into Hull House at 335 Halsted Street. A housekeeper, Mary Keyser, moved in at the same time. Jane Addams had begun her life's work just twelve days after her twenty-ninth birthday.

"The streets are inexpressibly dirty," Addams told a friend shortly after settling in. She added, "the number of schools [is] inadequate, sanitary legislation unenforced, the street lighting bad, the paving miserable . . . and the stables foul beyond description."[3] Nevertheless, she and her companions joyfully—and with great anticipation—awaited the venture just beginning.

Chapter 7

BEING A GOOD NEIGHBOR

hen she awoke the morning after her first night at Hull House, Addams realized she had left a side door unlocked—and wide open! Anyone could have come in and taken her expensive things. To her surprise, nothing had been touched. All the photos, silver, and other treasures were in the same place they had been left.

This incident made her feel safe in her new home. Neighbors, however, seemed suspicious of Addams and Starr and wondered why they had come to the neighborhood. The local residents had nothing in common with these two well-dressed women. These "do-gooders" had probably come to make fun of them.

The Neighbors Come Calling

Before long, one neighbor's curiosity got the best of her, and she knocked timidly on the Hull House door. The young woman, who was English, poured her heart out to Addams and Starr about the hard time she and her mother had had in America. Their plans to live with a relative in Chicago had not worked out, and since they had little money, they did not know what to do. Addams and Starr listened sympathetically, wondering how they could help their first visitor. For the young woman just to have a listening ear comforted her immensely. Soon she brought her mother to call at Hull House, much to the delight of Addams and Starr.

Other neighbors soon began to visit: Italian, Polish, German, Irish, and Russian immigrants came by—largely, at first, out of curiosity. Addams was thrilled. People from nearly all the countries she had visited in Europe were now visiting her! And she did not even have to leave the Nineteenth Ward of Chicago.

One day, another visitor came to Hull House. When Addams opened the door, she found a young Italian woman, who held a baby in her arms while a shy three-year-old tried to hide behind her skirts.

"I don't know what to do!" the woman told Addams anxiously in Italian. "I daren't leave the children alone. The friend who usually stays with them is awfully sick and if I'm late, I'll lose my job!"[1] Addams was thankful she could understand the woman's Italian mixed with a smattering of broken English. Her years studying languages in Europe had not been wasted. Addams told the young mother they would be delighted to help by keeping the children at Hull House.

The Children's Work

Other people also began to call on the two well-dressed women who lived in the old Hull mansion. A number of them had young children. Before long, Addams and Starr realized they needed to make provisions for the children, so they could not only play but also learn new things.

Starr remembered a friend of hers, Jenny Dow, who knew how to teach and work with children. When Dow arrived as a volunteer, she quickly organized a kindergarten class in the largest room. In a month's time, twenty-four children were attending the kindergarten, and at least seventy more were on the waiting list, since many rooms in Hull House had already been filled to capacity.

Older children also began to come to Hull House. Addams and her friends started groups and classes for them as well. They also organized clubs for young working men and women where they could take classes to learn about some current topic, or simply discuss problems and concerns about their jobs and families. They also started the Young Heroes Club, designed to get young boys off the streets. The boys belonging to this club played pool and chess, and listened to stories.

Because she remembered her own happy childhood days in Cedarville, Addams especially wanted to help the children who came to Hull House. She wished that they, too, could enjoy the green fields and hills of Cedarville. She recalled the wonderful games she had played with George, running and hiding in the mill and its surroundings. She realized that these city children had no place to play. In the back of her mind, a solution was beginning to form to give these children, too, a decent place to play.

Planning a special Christmas celebration, Addams purchased books about Abraham Lincoln for the boys' club, shoes for a few of the more destitute neighbors, and candy for the children. As her visitors arrived for the festivities, she noticed that a number of little girls turned their noses up at the candy. They appeared to hate even being around it!

When they told Addams they worked fourteen hours a day in a candy factory, she was appalled. No wonder the sight of candy made them ill. Addams had known that her neighbors were overworked and underpaid, but she had not known about the severity of child labor. And she had not been aware that many immigrant families counted on the money their children earned. Addams understood for the first time that she had known nothing of real poverty before she came to Hull House. She had wanted to provide art and beauty for the people. Now she realized that their need for simple sustenance was far greater.

Older people in the area had needs, too. Sometimes they were unable to go to work because of sickness, but they were also lonely and wanted someone to talk to. They had left their homes in Europe and come to America, where hardly anyone spoke their native language. To help these people, Addams decided to have an "Old Settlers' Party" on January 1, 1890. At the party, the older neighbors could meet new people, make friends, and just enjoy the gracious hospitality of Hull House. People had such a good time that the party became an annual event, with old-timers who had moved away from Chicago coming back to share their tales of prosperity and success.

It seemed that there was always something to do, something to take up the time of Hull House's residents: Perhaps there was a neighbor to talk to, a child to care for, a person who needed help. Not long after it opened, a few others besides Addams and Starr moved into Hull House, including Julia Lathrop, Florence Kelley, and Dr. Alice Hamilton. These women stayed a short time, then others came—all on a volunteer basis.

Many of these volunteers were young college women who needed a place to use their skills and expertise. Addams believed Hull House was the perfect place for many of these women to put their education into practice. They took care of the children, taught English and other classes, guided the clubs, and enjoyed tea and conversation with the neighbors who stopped by.

Oddly enough, some neighbors continued to be suspicious of the goings-on at Hull House. Over and over Addams was

Urban Ghetto

Urban ghettoes are sections of a city occupied by a minority group living there because of social, economic, or legal pressure. In the nineteenth-century Chicago urban ghetto, the people lived in a "noxious atmosphere compounded of decaying food, stagnant water, primitive sewage, and coal soot. In summer, the heat seared their bodies; in winter, the cold chilled their bones; and their weakened physical condition left them vulnerable to tuberculosis and pneumonia." Usually they could not afford a doctor, so the ill simply lay on filthy beds until death removed them from their misery.[2]

asked why she had come to Hull House. One old man shook his head and said it was "the strangest thing he had met in his experience." Later, he admitted it was "not strange but natural."[3] As far as Addams could tell, to feed the hungry and tend the sick, to give pleasure to the young and comfort to the aged, and to provide human warmth and kindness to all people, seemed more than natural.

Chapter 8

EXPANDING VISION

The neighbors continued to come to Hull House. They sought fellowship, most of all, but also someone to care about them, and someone to help with their problems. To Addams, it was not enough simply to express concern for other people; it was necessary to do all one could to benefit and help them.

Given the many needs of the people of the area, Addams seldom knew what would be required of her each day. Early one morning, she received an urgent message. Not far from Hull House, an old German woman, who had no money to pay her bills, was resisting being taken to the poorhouse. In sheer terror and fright, she hung on to her dresser with all her strength. She did not want to leave her home and familiar surroundings!

As Addams spoke calmly to her with compassion, the old woman let go of the dresser. Then Addams talked with the officials who had come to take the old woman away, telling them that she and some of the neighbors would take care of the woman. The officials agreed, and the woman was allowed to stay in her own home.[1] Addams and some of the other Hull House volunteers started coming to visit the old woman, bringing her food and materials she could use to do handwork, and simply talking with her. From then on, the woman responded to the attention from Addams and her coworkers. The city officials were satisfied with the outcome.

Another incident showing Addams's kindness occurred one night after she had gone to bed. She awoke suddenly, disturbed by a shadowy figure moving across the room. Even though she knew the person was a burglar, she was not afraid.

"Don't make a noise," she whispered. When the startled burglar began to leave the way he had come—through the window—she urged him to use the door instead, since it would be much safer than leaving from a second-story window. Without a word, the would-be thief tiptoed down the stairs and went out the front door.[2] A later burglar, also surprised by Addams, was offered an honest job if he returned in the morning. He did—and Addams found a job for him.

Hull House Grows

The financial demands on Hull House often exceeded the supply of available funds. This situation led Addams to look beyond Hull House for assistance. She began speaking to wealthy people around Chicago who were interested in her work. Some great encouragement came from her landlady, Helen Culver. In 1890, Culver donated all of Hull House, as well as some surrounding land, rent-free for four years. This generous gift allowed for some badly needed expansion.

The first building project for Hull House was an art gallery, built in 1891. Since Addams always wanted to enrich people's lives with art and beauty, this new addition made her dream possible. Coming at all hours to see the paintings and to read in the cozy library, working people were delighted with the gallery. Their drab lives often had no room for beautiful pictures or good reading material.

Addams recognized the need for beauty to enrich people's lives. One incident in particular impressed her about this need. An Italian woman attending a Hull House reception seemed pleased to see an arrangement of fresh red roses. She expressed surprise, however, that they had been "brought so fresh all the way from Italy."[3] She simply could not believe that they had been grown in America. She had lived in Chicago six years but had never seen any roses. In Italy, she said, there were always roses in the summer. During the time she had lived in Chicago, a florist shop and a city park existed just a few blocks away. The woman's ignorance of American ways and language had kept her handicapped in her understanding of the city.

Many Uses

Hull House served people in various ways. To some, it became a home away from home. As one immigrant explained,

> Our family lived in four small rooms. Half the week, during the winter; the rooms were filled with laundry. Since the clothes were all wrung by hand, it took several days to get the clothes dry. It was no place in which to entertain friends, so while I ate and slept there, I really lived at Hull-House.[4]

Other immigrants enjoyed Hull House for different reasons. One neighbor, Mary Kenney, who worked for a book bindery, told Addams that the bookbinders' group Kenney had organized lacked a decent meeting place. Currently, they were meeting over a saloon. When Addams invited them to meet at Hull House, Kenney was overcome with gratitude. She wrote to a friend later, "When I saw there was someone who cared enough to help us in our way, it was like having a new world opened up."[5]

New Opportunities and Volunteers

Now the growth of Hull House began to speed up. After the art gallery was built, several new helpers arrived. One of them, Louise de Koven Bowen, built Bowen Hall for the Women's Club. Another volunteer, Mary Rozet Smith, made her home available for Addams, Starr, and their coworkers. None of these volunteers received wages of any kind. Most of them were independently wealthy and were thankful for the opportunities they had to help others by working at Hull House.

Each of these women volunteers—followed later by several others—brought her own knowledge, skill, and wisdom to Hull House. For example, Mary Rozet Smith's quiet manner calmed many troubled situations. Fluent in several languages and gifted in music, Smith organized the early music clubs for children. She also had an ability to find talented children and helped them get training in their areas of interest. She never lived at Hull House but worked many hours there, giving her time and service.

Three others—Julia Lathrop, Florence Kelley, and Dr. Alice Hamilton—came to Hull House because of their interests in children, housing, and public health. Julia Lathrop knew much about legal matters, which was quite unusual for a woman of that day. Lathrop was from Rockford, Illinois, where her father was a successful attorney. She turned out to be a valuable asset to Hull House with her expert knowledge in legal affairs. Lathrop later received an appointment to two offices: as official visitor for Cook County's poor people and as a member of the State Board of Charities. In Lathrop's position as official visitor, she reported to the city on the condition of the poor in the Hull House neighborhood. She found the people suffering many abuses, the last indignity being death and burial without any religious services, including, perhaps, burial in a pauper's grave (where a person is buried if he or she has no money at the time of death).

Lathrop also played a part in establishing the Juvenile Court in Cook County—the first in the nation; and she was appointed to head the Federal Children's Bureau in Washington, D.C. Established by Congress in 1912, the bureau concerned itself with the care and welfare of the country's dependent children.

Cornell-educated Florence Kelley was from Philadelphia. She had traveled widely and spoke several languages. Her interests lay in improving labor conditions in the miserable sweatshops. People worked long hours in sweatshops, which were suffocating in the summer and freezing in the winter. Often, wealthy and middle-income people purchased the clothing made in the sweatshops but did not realize where their garments had been made. Slowly, partly as a result of Kelley's efforts, conditions in the factories began to improve.[6]

Dr. Alice Hamilton contributed some important services to Hull House. She had a medical degree from the University of Michigan and had studied at Johns Hopkins University. Although she taught at a medical college and did research on industrial medicine at Rush medical laboratories, she came to Hull House regularly, doing medical studies on issues such as how often workers became sick because of poor job conditions. She also treated old people and babies for their physical problems.

Chicago's Playground

Addams had been troubled for some time about the lack of outdoor places for children to play. She did not know what to do about it until a young businessman, William Kent, offered her some old, run-down apartment buildings. He had recently inherited the buildings and did not know about their condition. Kent thought perhaps Hull House could put them to use. Addams asked instead that they be torn down. Kent refused at first, but then realized she wanted them torn down for her neighbors, not for herself. After he agreed to her terms, she asked

Sweatshop

A sweatshop is a shop or factory in which employees work long hours at low wages under poor and dirty conditions doing work that may be difficult or dangerous. It is a workplace that has socially unacceptable working conditions. Sweatshops operated and thrived in big cities in the late 1800s and early 1900s. By the mid-1930s and beyond, new labor laws had been passed, outlawing sweatshop conditions. However, sweatshops still exist in some Caribbean and Asian countries, and in various other developing areas around the world.

him if he would purchase playground equipment for the now-vacant lots. Before long, she saw energetic, happy children swinging on swings, coming down the slide, and digging in the sandbox! She was glad she had persuaded Kent to tear down the buildings and put a playground in their place. The Hull House playground was the only one in Chicago at that time.[7]

The Word Spreads

Within a few years, Jane Addams realized that people in many different places wanted to hear about Hull House. As she traveled to different cities and states—and even foreign countries later on—she gave speeches on health and housing; on children and their need to be educated and provided for; on the immigrant people pouring into American cities; on clean streets, decent wages, and good working conditions. Though Addams did not consider herself a public speaker, her earnest desire to talk of people's needs and what Hull House was doing won her ready audiences everywhere.

The wealthy people to whom Addams spoke generally knew nothing of slum conditions in their cities. Addams taught them. Soon, many wanted to help, if only through financial gifts. Her listeners were fascinated with the stories Addams told them about Hull House. She told them stories like the one about Theo, a young boy from Greece. One day as Addams came back to Hull House, Theo met her. Excitedly, he showed her his new shoes, bending down and running his finger over the shoe tops. She agreed that they were beautiful.

"Ain't they *nice*? I never had *new* American shoes before. My father is working steady now and he says he can get one of us kids a pair each pay-day. Nida gets hers next. Ain't they wonderful?" The glow in his face showed his pride and joy.[8] Stories like these appealed to Addams's audiences and encouraged them to contribute time or money toward continuing Hull House's success.

Other Influences

As Jane Addams spoke and wrote about Hull House and its activities, the news of what was going on there spread far and wide. Even Russian novelist Leo Tolstoy had heard of Addams. She had her chance to meet him in 1896 when she took her first long vacation in years.

She was not prepared for the rebuke he gave her. A rich man who belonged to Russia's noble class, Tolstoy had renounced his position and wealth and made a decision to live among the extremely poor Russian serfs. When Tolstoy and Addams met, he chided her for the extra fabric in her garment, saying that the surplus would easily make a coat for a little girl. Learning that she earned some income from an Illinois farm her father had left her, Tolstoy called her an absentee landlord. He thought she should work on the farm herself. Finally, Tolstoy suggested that she do the housework herself at Hull House. Little did he realize that by this time, Hull House amounted to nearly an entire city block!

Wisely, Addams applied what she could to her situation from Tolstoy and put the rest of his ideas aside, realizing that what worked for Tolstoy in Russia could never apply to the bustling city of Chicago. Addams appreciated the visit but knew that she and Tolstoy were worlds apart.[9]

Chapter 9

WORKING FOR SOCIAL JUSTICE

S ome of the people who visited Hull House, like Florence Kelley and Julia Lathrop, decided to stay. As they learned of people's needs, they were able to work for reforms in those areas. Florence Kelley was interested in social reform. She and Addams began to study the way people lived and worked in Chicago's Nineteenth Ward, where Hull House was located.

Better Laws

Even though Kelley and Addams already knew much about their neighborhood, they needed to pass facts and figures on to lawmakers. They compiled information on the number of different nationalities in their neighborhood, the total population, and how many children held jobs.

Child Labor

Kelley persuaded Addams to work toward changing the child labor laws. Through Kelley's efforts, legislation to stop employers from hiring children under the age of fourteen came before the

Illinois state legislature in 1893. Kelley and Addams worked hard to make it become law. For three months, Addams spoke nearly every night to clubs, church groups, and trade unions. To work all day, then speak every night proved exhausting. But Addams thought of the children's terrible working conditions and long hours. Maybe she could put a stop to their wearisome jobs.

Some children worked over sixty hours a week in factories. Other very young children were forced to work at home with their mothers on garments brought home from sweatshops. In this work, called piecework, laborers were paid according to how much they got done, instead of being paid for their time. After bending over their sewing for hours in airless, dimly lit rooms, women would often bring their work home, where their children would help them. Florence Kelley noted that "From the age of eighteen months few children able to sit in high chairs at tables were safe from being required to pull basting threads."[1]

In 1893, the Factory Act was passed by the Illinois state legislature, which prohibited children from working more than eight hours a day. Some people resented the new law. Factory owners and managers who depended on child laborers because of their low wages were irritated with people like Addams and Kelley. These factory managers wanted them to mind their own affairs. Much to the chagrin of Kelley and Addams, the Factory Act was repealed in 1895 because of intense opposition by these factory managers and others who profited from child labor. Though disappointed, Addams and Kelley continued their fight for new and better child labor laws.

Other Reforms

Julia Lathrop was concerned about young people arrested for minor offenses being tried like hardened criminals. The Juvenile Court she helped establish tried to reform young people instead of merely punishing them. She also conducted a study of conditions in mental hospitals and county poorhouses to see how these could be improved.

Ellen Starr, too, was involved in projects. She opened a bookbindery at Hull House and started the Chicago Public School Art Society. Through her efforts, young, educated women came to help at Hull House. Starr also concerned herself with the unionization of working women and campaigned tirelessly— even participating in strikes and picket lines—for this cause.

Addams herself worked for many causes—big and small. One of the important ways she helped people was to bring about better employment agencies. Many of the existing agencies were dishonest, promising the people who applied better jobs with more money, then failing to provide what they promised—after the applicants had paid the agency a fee for finding them a new job. Hull House volunteers helped their neighbors work through the good agencies while they discredited the bad ones. Addams and her coworkers also oversaw a state bill, passed in 1899, ordering the inspection of all employment agencies by the government.[2]

Another need filled by Addams and the Hull House staff was for their own post office. When immigrants tried to send cash to their families in Europe, dishonest postal clerks often charged high fees for obtaining money orders at the city post office, or they simply stole the money entrusted to them. Once Hull House set up its own post office—Sub-Station Number 10—the immigrants could safely entrust their money to the postal clerks.[3]

Incorporation

By 1894, Addams and Starr knew they could no longer support Hull House and its many activities on their incomes alone. Addams had received money from her father's estate, which

John Dewey (1859-1952)

An American philosopher and educator, John Dewey was a leading teacher of pragmatism, or practicality. Dewey's philosophy of education used a method that started with a child's real problems and experience and then taught the child from that foundation. Dewey's ideas and methods have been very influential in American education.

could support her but not Hull House. So they decided to incorporate, setting up a board of trustees to oversee Hull House's operations and activities. These trustees, one of whom was famed educator John Dewey, provided advice as well as financial support to Hull House. Included in the articles of incorporation was the goal "to investigate and improve the conditions in the industrial districts of Chicago."[4]

As Addams's chances to speak increased, she shared her vision of Hull House and its activities . She spoke about the Hull House staff's reaching out to meet their neighbors' needs. She spoke of not only their successes, but also the challenges. Because the idea of a settlement house was new to most Americans, Addams told them about immigrant needs and how they could be addressed. Addams also discussed the wretched conditions of the cities. She urged her audiences to help her in changing these conditions.

The Pullman Strike

Addams tried to stay close to her family, visiting whenever she could and writing frequent letters. However, in 1894, she was caught between her family and the disastrous Pullman railroad strike that began in May.

Addams's sister Mary had been seriously ill for some time, and in July 1894, Addams wanted to go see her. Angry railroad strikers, however, had vowed to stop railroad travel across the country. Addams had been asked by a citizens' group to help settle the strike. What should she do? Suddenly, she was torn between her family and her work.

The striking workers, employed by the Pullman Palace Car Company, made sleeping cars for the railroads. Unlike the people who lived near Hull House, many of the striking workers had nice homes. Their employer, George Pullman, had built an entire town for them, so they enjoyed stores, schools, a library, and even gyms. However, the workers had no choice but to live there and pay high rents. They were also required to do all their shopping at the town stores. When their employer reduced wages but did not lower rents, the workers went on strike. To show their support for the Pullman workers, the railroad union also voted to strike and refused to operate trains carrying Pullman cars.

Acting as a mediator, Addams visited some of the workers in their homes and even spoke with George Pullman. Pullman, however, refused to enter into mediation. He believed he could run his business any way he saw fit. Addams also attended a number of the strikers' meetings, but nothing she or anyone else did changed the circumstances, and the strike continued.

Addams finally took a carriage to visit Mary in July, but realized that other family members could not see Mary because the trains were not running as usual. When Mary died, shortly after Addams's arrival, Addams returned to Chicago. She had been gone a few weeks, and the strike was still going on. Both sides refused to budge, but Pullman could hold out longer than the workers. Federal troops finally broke up the strike, though none of the issues were settled. None of the striking Pullman workers returned to work for the Pullman Palace Car Company, and they found it difficult to find employment elsewhere.

The Reform Movement

The desire to bring her sister Mary's son, Stanley, who was nearly eleven, to live in Chicago caused Addams to be concerned about something in addition to improving working conditions and helping the poor. Doctors told her it was not safe for Stanley on the Chicago streets. The lack of safety had little to do with violence: It had to do with garbage piled in the streets. Addams had lived in Hull House over five years, and garbage had continued to pile up. Filthy rags and rotting fruits and vegetables covered the pavement, and children played in and around the huge garbage boxes. They would hide in the boxes, then reach inside for a piece of refuse to toss at their friends. The terrible odor of rotting garbage made some people ill, particularly during the humid summer months. The decaying garbage also posed a constant threat of disease.

Although Addams had reported the situation to city hall many times, little was done to remove the garbage. Addams tried to teach her neighbors to keep their children away from the trash, to wash their hands often, and to protect their food from flies. Nevertheless, flies and rats bred in the garbage heaps.

Addams knew she could protect her nephew by sending him to a safe, clean school away from the city—but what about the neighborhood children who had no such privileges? Now she sensed a new determination. She would confront city hall and get the situation changed. She would have clean streets.

First of all, Addams looked at the private trash collectors. She found that they were more interested in getting paid than in doing their jobs properly. Next, she got other neighborhood women involved to see what laws were being broken in regard to garbage collection. Within two months, the women discovered not only many dangerous practices, but also over a thousand health law violations.[5]

Confronting city hall with the violations, Addams said she would remove the garbage herself, but her request was refused. Instead, the mayor appointed her garbage inspector for her neighborhood, the Nineteenth Ward. It was the only paying job she ever had. Addams would rise at daybreak and climb into a horse-drawn wagon. Wearing a fresh white blouse and a long skirt, Addams must have looked out of place as she followed the garbage collectors down the filthy streets. But she was a tough and very determined inspector.[6]

Earlier garbage inspectors would let garbage pile up on the sidewalks, and no one questioned them. Probably Chicago's best garbage inspector, Addams was a stickler with the trash collectors. She made them pick up trash that fell from the wagons and insisted that they add more wagons if necessary to collect all the garbage. When landlords did not have enough garbage containers for their tenants, she reported them to the authorities. She also insisted that dead animals be removed from the streets.

After she had been a garbage inspector for less than a year, Addams reported to the Hull House Woman's Club that the Nineteenth Ward no longer had the third highest death rate in Chicago. Its rank had fallen to seventh place. The women applauded the news enthusiastically. Though she still wanted a lower death rate and cleaner streets, Addams's efforts had paid off.

By now, Addams had lived at Hull House for ten years and had been active in many areas. Hull House had grown and included additional buildings. It now boasted an art gallery, a gymnasium, a children's house, a music school, a new building for the Jane Club (a residence for working women), a coffeehouse, a theater, and apartments for men and women. Besides these additions, the meeting rooms overflowed with people attending clubs and classes. The people who lived at Hull House were kept continually busy overseeing clubs, classes, and other activities, meeting new people, and conducting neighborhood studies.

Addams, too, had grown and changed. She was happy reaching out to people as she had longed to do all her life. Now, Hull House was about to enter its second decade serving its neighbors—and reaching far beyond its own boundaries.

Chapter 10

ACHIEVEMENTS
AND LEGACY

As Addams sat on her porch in the spring of 1900, she felt somewhat satisfied with what she had accomplished. The classes and clubs were well attended, and many people were helping to support Hull House. Still, she was troubled as she watched people pass by. The older generation of immigrants often dressed in their native costumes while the younger generation always wore American clothes.

Living Museum

Thinking about the rapid Americanization of the young, Addams realized that many of the customs and crafts brought over from Europe would soon disappear as the older generation passed on. The thought came to her of setting up a museum where immigrants could practice their arts, crafts, and other traditions, and demonstrate them to others.

A short time later, as Addams walked down Polk Street, she saw an old Italian woman sitting on the shabby tenement steps, spinning yarn. The old woman's threadbare shawl hung far down on her gaunt shoulders. But her nimble fingers moved quickly across the handmade loom. The woman spun yarn in the simplest of ways a method used by peasants for hundreds of years in her native country. Most likely, her own children and grandchildren in America worked in factories. Perhaps they were unable to spin yarn like this woman did. Addams made up her mind. She would have people like this old woman come to Hull House regularly and work at their crafts—spinning, weaving, or any other traditional type of craft. That way, the younger generation could watch and learn from them. Maybe such traditional work would not be lost after all.

In a month's time, Addams had a room prepared at Hull House for her Living Museum—where people demonstrated their various skills. Then, she scoured the neighborhood, looking for people to work in the museum. She located several women skilled in different ways of spinning wool and weaving cloth. She also found people who could teach wood carving, painting, and pottery making. Before long, the Hull House Living Museum was ready for its grand opening.

Sometime after the museum opened, a young woman named Angelina came to talk to Addams. To her surprise, Angelina noticed several important visitors watching her mother spin on her loom in the Living Museum. They admired the older woman's skill, and Angelina suddenly felt very proud of her mother.

An immigrant from Ireland named Francis Hackett later recalled why Hull House was so special to him. He said that "Hull-House was American because it was international and because it was perceived that the nationalism of each immigrant was a treasure, a talent, which gave him a special value for the United States."[1]

Opposition and Crises

Addams had enjoyed a growing popularity by 1901. Hull House had become known in many places all over the world, providing a good example of what a settlement house should be. Other settlements had sprung up in New York, Boston, and in other major cities. An incident occurred in 1901, however, that altered many people's view of Addams. President William McKinley had been shot by an anarchist who considered the government too powerful. Before long, anyone who disagreed with government policies was considered radical and dangerous to the nation. Many innocent people, especially immigrants, were arrested in Chicago merely because of their foreign ideas. A newspaper editor and political radical named Abraham Isaak was arrested. Other Russian Jewish immigrants were outraged.

Even though his supporters knew that Isaak's newspaper printed views that sometimes disagreed with the government, they did not believe he should be arrested for his political beliefs alone. His supporters went to Jane Addams and complained about Isaak's arrest.

Addams asked Chicago's mayor, Edward F. Dunne, for permission to visit Isaak. A social worker accompanied Addams when she visited Isaak in his dingy cell beneath city hall. Isaak was nervous and frightened but apparently unharmed. Unable to get him released, Addams at least told his family and friends that he was all right.

When Isaak's release finally came, people thought Addams had brought it about and reacted negatively to her. Some even threw rocks through Hull House's windows. Addams's and Hull House's popularity had begun to wane.

The following year, a former Illinois governor and old friend of Addams's, John P. Altgeld, died. He had taken some very unpopular stands while he was governor, which included reducing child labor and bringing about shorter working hours for women. He and Addams had worked closely together on these issues. Of course, because of Altgeld's position on these matters, corporate leaders and factory owners disliked him. After his term as governor ended, he never ran for another political office.

When Altgeld's body lay in state in the Chicago Public Library, thousands of people passed by his coffin to pay their last respects. These were mostly humble people whom Altgeld had helped in one way or another. At his funeral, only a few people spoke to praise him for his accomplishments. Among them were Dr. Frank Crane, his minister; Clarence Darrow, his law partner; and Jane Addams. Addams's friends believed that her speaking at Altgeld's funeral would cause further erosion in Hull House's (and Addams's) popularity. Altgeld's funeral would signal the final blow to Hull House's influence and the financial support it enjoyed. But Addams had never been easily swayed from doing what she believed to be right, so she did speak at Altgeld's funeral, after which several prominent people withdrew their support from Hull House.

Despite the backlash from Addams's seeing Isaak and speaking at Altgeld's funeral, she soon found an extremely important ally—the president of the United States, Theodore Roosevelt. President Roosevelt first encountered Jane Addams's name when he was governor of New York. He, too, was concerned with the clearing of slums. He looked with interest at what Addams was doing at Hull House. As a result, whenever Roosevelt was in the city of Chicago, he made it a point to visit Hull House and discuss politics and reform needs with Addams. The two became good friends.

Hull House Expansion

Addams's relationship with Roosevelt helped dismiss some of the earlier ill will against her. In spite of some loss of revenue, the settlement house continued to prosper. By 1902, an apartment building with a men's club was completed, followed by a residents' dining hall and the Boys' Club building. It seemed something exciting was always going on at Hull House! Old buildings were either being remodeled or moved to meet changing needs while new ones were being built alongside the old. With the completion of a new children's nursery in 1907, Hull House was made up of thirteen interconnected buildings that covered an entire city block.

Not only did Hull House grow and expand, but so did Addams's opportunities to speak and write. She knew that she could spread her ideas most effectively through writing. Having kept a thorough record of her speeches, Addams now set about writing them down and polishing them. Always very careful, she revised her talks and reviewed them cautiously to be sure each was just right.

Addams's autobiography, *Twenty Years at Hull-House*, sold many copies. In it, Addams told of her happy childhood in Cedarville, Illinois; of her college years at Rockford Female Seminary; and in particular, about the close relationship she had had with her father and how deeply his death had affected her. She also shared her feelings about her first glimpses of poverty and about Mile End Road in London. Of course, Jane Addams also wrote much about her work at Hull House, the people who lived there and had lived there, and the people who came to visit, to take classes or to do volunteer work. *Twenty Years at Hull-House* was first published in 1910, the year Addams celebrated her fiftieth birthday.

Honors and Recognition

By now, Addams had changed considerably from the insecure young girl who did not know what to do with her life. At fifty, she was calm and poised, possessing maturity and confidence. She seemed stern and remote at times, but those who knew her realized that underneath a rather foreboding exterior, she was kind and considerate. In addition, Addams relied on an inner spiritual strength and had an excellent business mind. No matter how many things she needed to do on any day, Addams could always find time to help someone in need.

One of the best-known women in America by 1910, Addams's outstanding work had not gone unnoticed by others. She turned her attention increasingly to larger, worldwide causes, and received the honor of being named the first woman president of the National Conference of Charities and Corrections. Receiving honorary degrees from Yale University and Smith College, Addams was even considered as a possible senatorial candidate—although not too seriously, since women could not even vote!

Suffrage and Peace

Addams had long been interested in women's rights. In 1906, she attended her first meeting of the National American Woman Suffrage Association (NAWSA), a group promoting the right to vote for women. At that time, she met Susan B. Anthony, one of the leaders in the women's suffrage movement. Addams gave a speech explaining why women should be able to vote. Addams's life in the Nineteenth Ward proved to her that if women could vote, they could correct many of the city's evils.

By 1911, NAWSA had elected Addams its vice president, and the following year, she spoke at its convention in Philadelphia. Following the convention, she went to Washington, D.C., to tell Congress why women should have the right to vote. She told

Suffragette

Women who identified with the late nineteenth- and early twentieth-century movement in England and the United States to secure voting rights for women were known as suffragists, or suffragettes. (Suffragette was a British term often applied to American women with a negative tone. Most American suffrage leaders preferred to be called suffragists.) Women won the vote in the United States in 1920. In England, however, women's voting rights were not achieved until in 1929, when women over the age of twenty-one could vote.

them that being a wife and mother and running a home was similar to running the country—only on a smaller scale.[2] Despite her efforts, Congress refused to grant women voting rights at that time.

When Theodore Roosevelt ran for president again as a third-party candidate in 1912, he endorsed some of the social and factory reforms that Addams and her Hull House coworkers supported. Since Addams and Roosevelt had become good friends, she willingly backed his party—with one exception. She disagreed with his position of not involving African Americans in the Progressive party convention. Addams had helped found the new National Association for the Advancement of Colored People (NAACP), even though not many African Americans lived near Hull House.

Despite her disagreement with Roosevelt's racial position, Addams took part in the Progressive party campaign and gave one of the party nomination speeches in favor of Roosevelt. As she spoke, people listened attentively: "A great party has pledged itself to the protection of children, to the care of the aged, the relief of overworked girls, the safeguarding of burdened men." Addams's quiet manner assured the crowd that their goals were one and the same—and they heartily applauded her.[3]

Working for World Peace

Nearly two years after Roosevelt's campaign and subsequent defeat, Addams became involved in another struggle—the struggle for peace. When World War I erupted in Europe in August 1914, Addams and Mary Rozet Smith were vacationing at their summer home in Bar Harbor, Maine. With their peaceful surroundings, the war seemed unreal and far away. The causes for the war were numerous, but it was sparked by the assassination of Archduke Franz Ferdinand of Austria and his wife at Sarajevo in Bosnia on June 28, 1914. Austria declared war on Serbia, Russia sided with Serbia, and Germany declared war on Russia. The German invasion of neutral Belgium brought Great Britain into the war on the French side. Soon Japan joined Great Britain, France, and Russia, forming the Allied forces. Italy joined the Allies in May 1915. In November 1914, Turkey sided with Germany and was joined by Bulgaria in October 1915.

As the news continued to reach the United States about young men fighting and being killed in Europe, Addams became more and more concerned. What could she do to prevent such a waste of human life? The United States had not yet become involved in the war, and she resolved to do what she could to keep her country from entering it, and to work toward a peaceful solution. Addams had always been an advocate of peace, and some years earlier she had expressed her views in a book called *Newer Ideals of Peace*. She called herself a pacifist, and in her book she declared that war should be completely done away with. She received much criticism for her stand on peace and for her objection to the United States' entering the war in Europe.[4]

Then, on January 15, 1915, a conference of various women's groups was held in Washington, D.C. A new, unified group known as the Woman's Peace Party came out of the conference and elected Jane Addams as its head.

Before long, a movement known as the International Congress of Women was formed among women worldwide to promote peace. These women met at The Hague in the Netherlands, and once again, they asked Jane Addams to be their leader. There were a thousand official delegates from twelve nations, but sometimes at least another thousand people participated in the meetings. The Congress voted to urge the warring nations to call a conference of neutral nations to offer mediation in the hope of ending the war. Addams also tried to persuade President Woodrow Wilson to initiate mediation, but she met with little success.

Other strategies toward achieving peace came out of the conference, but before the women could try them, German submarines sank the British ship *Lusitania*. Over one hundred Americans were on the ship, and many of them were killed. Now more and more Americans wanted the United States to declare war. In April 1917, the United States entered the war on the side of the Allies. Soon every effort was being made to win it.

People often misunderstood Addams's efforts to promote peace, and for a time, she became unpopular. Because Addams wanted the United States to stay out of the war, groups like the Daughters of the American Revolution (DAR) and the American Legion disagreed with her. In fact, the DAR expelled her from membership. She appeared unpatriotic—even pro-German—to many of the American people. To justify her view, Addams gave a speech called "Patriotism and Pacifists in Wartime." Addams stated, "The position of the pacifist in time of war is most difficult, and necessarily he must abandon the perfectly legitimate

Pacifism

Pacifism refers to the doctrine of opposition to all wars, including civil wars. Pacifists support efforts to maintain peace and advocate disarmament, especially through the strengthening of international organizations and law. They have long been associated with Christian sects, but in the twentieth century they include many who oppose war from secular moral bases. Pacifism is often associated with support for nonviolent political action.

propaganda he maintained before war was declared."[5] Her views were unacceptable to many people who had prowar views.

In 1918, Germany launched a major attack in the spring but was driven back by the Allies. Soon, the Germans began a full-scale retreat and surrendered. In November 1918, all warring parties signed an armistice, or declaration of peace.

After the war, in April 1919, Addams, Lillian Wald, Jeanette Rankin, and Dr. Alice Hamilton traveled through Europe on their way to the second International Congress of Women in Zurich, Switzerland. Addams was dismayed at the destruction she saw at every turn. Traveling through Germany, they saw starving children everywhere—children with "little sticklike legs, the swollen bellies, the ribs one could count, the shoulder blades sticking out like wings," according to Hamilton.[6] Returning to the United States, Addams urged Americans to help the people of Germany. Many people criticized her views, and she was even called a traitor by some. People could not understand Addams's desire to help all people, wherever they lived. People refused to believe the children in their former enemy's country were actually starving, so they considered Addams an enemy sympathizer.

Throughout the 1920s, Addams continued to work for world peace through an organization called the Women's International League for Peace and Freedom. Although still involved with Hull House, the world had become her forum. In 1922, Addams and her close friend Mary Rozet Smith traveled around the world. Everywhere they went, Addams was acclaimed. Japanese schoolchildren greeted her with five thousand flags.[7]

Addams's health had never been good, but now she began to suffer from various ailments. In Japan, she had a benign breast tumor removed. Then in 1926, she suffered a heart attack. Despite these physical setbacks, she continued to travel the world, going to Prague, Czechoslovakia, for a conference of the

Women's International League. She greatly enjoyed these meetings but finally resigned her presidency because of poor health. The women gave her the title of honorary president.

Triumph and Achievement

The second volume of Addams's autobiography, *The Second Twenty Years at Hull-House*, was published in 1929. It described her views and work for peace and women's rights. It also told of the many changes in the Hull House neighborhood.

But now, Addams wanted to celebrate the forty years of Hull House's existence. Old-timers returned to take part, great dinners were prepared with foods from all over the world, and people gave speeches telling what Hull House had meant to them.

By the 1930s, Addams was once again receiving acclaim from the American people. In October 1929, the American stock market suddenly crashed. Many banks and businesses began to fail, throwing people out of work and setting off what would become known as the Great Depression. As economic conditions became worse in the United States, people began to remember all the good things Addams had done during the years before World War I. They especially remembered her work at Hull House in reaching out to poor people. Many people had forgotten her involvement in promoting peace during wartime, and she was praised and honored by many institutions. In 1931, she received her greatest honor, the Nobel Peace Prize, but because of a bronchitis attack and surgery for another tumor, she was unable to travel to Norway to accept it. The Nobel Committee had granted her the award because of her earlier efforts to promote peace. Despite the years of severe criticism she had faced because of her views on world peace, Addams was vindicated after all.

Addams lived the next few years of her life trying to help her neighbors and to make the world a safer, better place. In February 1935, Addams received the American Education Award and attended Washington, D.C., celebrations in her honor. She also addressed the world by radio. However, her health continued to fail. On May 21, 1935, she died from recently discovered intestinal cancer. She was seventy-four years old.

Jane Addams's funeral took place at Hull House as thousands of people gathered in the courtyard to pay their last respects. She was buried in the Cedarville Cemetery beside her father and mother. The marker on her gravestone reads simply: "JANE ADDAMS OF HULL-HOUSE AND THE WOMEN'S INTERNATIONAL LEAGUE FOR PEACE AND FREEDOM." The epitaph is a brief one for a person who accomplished so much throughout her lifetime, and for one who responded to each new challenge with courage and according to a sensitive conscience, fine-tuned from years of practice.

Chapter 11

AFTERWORD

As people gathered for Jane Addams's funeral service, one of her own little six-year-old grandnieces looked at the crowd and whispered, "Are we all Aunt Jane's children?"[1] In a real sense, the thousands of people gathered there, and many more around the world, were all "Aunt Jane's children." They had all benefited from her compassion, selflessness, influence, and example.

Of course, there were always those who were not happy with Addams—even some of Hull House's immigrant neighbors, who resented the programs as a form of social control. But the majority of Hull House visitors profited from their experiences learning in classes and attending many other activities.

Some have wondered what difference Hull House and the ideas it represents have made. What influence have the classes held there, the clubs, the musical programs, and all the other activities had? Perhaps only a few hundred people, overall, actually attended functions at Hull House. The others Addams influenced either read her writings or heard her speak. Addams's vision and ideas live on, however, not only in the people reached by the Hull House centers in Chicago, but in numerous other cities across the United States.

Addams worked hard to bring about change in people's lives. Sometimes, she was the only one who brought hope and friendship to certain people. As she became acquainted with her neighbors at Hull House, she adapted to their needs and responded with positive steps that improved their lives. She was just one person and could not solve everyone's problems. She could and did, however, help quite a few people.

From modest beginnings at Hull House, Addams helped to begin a whole movement—a movement that spread throughout society. Middle-class and wealthy people learned about the problems of the poor and immigrant people. They also learned that they could help remedy some of society's ills. Largely through Addams's efforts, people became aware not only of poor people's needs, but of what they could do to improve living conditions. After Addams's death in 1935, various government agencies began to meet many of the needs met earlier by places like Hull House. The next two decades also saw the professionalization of social work, which made the activities of Hull House seem less important.

Addams also paved the way for many college-educated young women who earlier had not known how to use their skills. She was able to show them that they could have an impact.

Still standing on Halsted Street, the original mansion that contained Hull House looks as gracious and dignified as ever. However, much of the old impoverished neighborhood of the Nineteenth Ward was torn down in 1963 and has been replaced by the campus of the University of Illinois at Chicago. Hull House is now a museum, having been restored to the way it looked when Addams lived there. Many of the other buildings added to Hull House over the years were torn down in 1963 to make room for the university. But Hull House survives at many other locations in the city of Chicago.

Addams was especially interested in the Women's International League for Peace and Freedom. That organization still carries on its work for human rights and peace around the world. The Hull House Association, begun in Addams's time, maintains its outreach to the poor with programs, organizations, and community centers around the Chicago area. Six neighborhood centers exist in Chicago. Using Addams's example, these centers feed, clothe, shelter, and counsel the needy. They also teach classes such as baby care, cooking, ballet, and sculpture. Unlike the neighbors of Jane Addams's day, the majority of the people who utilize Hull House programs today are no longer recent immigrants. Still, the boys, girls, men, and women who come to Hull House centers today are people of all nationalities and cultures. Addams would be pleased to know that the work she started continues to bring help and hope to people who would otherwise have none.

CHRONOLOGY

1860—Born on September 6, 1860, in Cedarville, Illinois.

1877—Begins to attend Rockford Female Seminary.

1881—Suffers severe depression after father's death.

1883—First European tour.

1889—Opens Hull House.

1896—Visits Leo Tolstoy in Russia.

1902—First book, *Democracy and Social Ethics*, published.

1907—Attends national peace conference; Joins woman suffrage committee.

1910—Receives honorary degree from Yale; Publishes *Twenty Years at Hull-House*.

1912—Campaigns for Theodore Roosevelt in presidential election.

1914—Attends International Suffrage Alliance in Budapest.

1915—Presides at The Hague over organization later called Women's International League for Peace and Freedom (WILPF).

1917—Opposes American entry into World War I.

1921—Presides over WILPF in Vienna.

1922—Records her relief work in *Peace and Bread in Time of War*.

1930—Publishes *The Second Twenty Years at Hull-House*.

1931—Wins Nobel Peace Prize.

1935—Wins American Education Award.

1935—Dies in Chicago on May 21.

CHAPTER NOTES

Chapter 1. The Nobel Peace Prize

1. James Weber Linn, *Jane Addams* (New York: D. Appleton-Century Company, Inc., 1935), p. 390.

2. Bernard S. Schlessinger and June Schlessinger, eds., *The Who's Who of Nobel Prize Winners* (Phoenix: The Oryx Press, 1986), p. 135.

3. Linn, p. 389.

4. Cornelia Meigs, *Jane Addams: Pioneer for Social Justice* (New York: Little, Brown & Company, 1970), pp. 256–257.

5. Ibid., p. 257.

6. Ibid., p. 256.

7. Ibid., p. 257.

Chapter 2. A Country Childhood

1. Marshall W. Fishwick et al., *Illustrious Americans: Jane Addams* (Morristown, N.J.: Silver Burdett Company, 1968), p. 9.

2. Cornelia Meigs, *Jane Addams: Pioneer for Social Justice* (New York: Little, Brown & Company, 1970), p. 5.

3. Jane Addams, *Twenty Years at Hull-House* (New York: The MacMillan Company, 1910), p. 2.

4. Addams, pp. 23–24.

5. Ibid.

6. Ibid., pp. 3–4.

7. Ibid., p. 7.

8. Ibid., p. 8.

9. Ibid., pp. 5–6.

10. Fishwick et al., p. 14.

11. Meigs, p. 17.

Chapter 3. The World Beyond Cedarville

1. Clara Ingram Judson, *City Neighbor: The Story of Jane Addams* (New York: Charles Scribner's Sons, 1951), pp. 20–21.

2. Ibid., p. 22.

3. Ibid., p. 23.

4. Ibid., p. 24.

5. Ibid.

6. Ibid., pp. 25–26.

7. Ibid., p. 26.

8. Cornelia Meigs, *Jane Addams: Pioneer for Social Justice* (New York: Little, Brown & Company, 1970), pp. 21–22.

9. Judson, pp. 28–30.

10. Meigs, pp. 23–24.

11. Ibid., pp. 31–32.

Chapter 4. A Change of Direction

1. Clara Ingram Judson, *City Neighbor: The Story of Jane Addams* (New York: Charles Scribner's Sons, 1951), p. 36.

2. Ibid., p. 37.

3. Ibid.

4. Marshall W. Fishwick et al., *Illustrious Americans: Jane Addams* (Morristown, N.J.: Silver Burdett Company, 1968), p. 33.

5. Ibid., p. 35.

6. Jane Addams, *Twenty Years at Hull-House* (New York: The MacMillan Company, 1910), pp. 67–68.

7. Judson, p. 42.

Chapter 5. Life's Work at Last

1. Cornelia Meigs, *Jane Addams: Pioneer for Social Justice* (New York: Little, Brown & Company, 1970), p. 39.

2. Stephanie Sammartino McPherson, *Peace and Bread: The Story of Jane Addams* (Minneapolis: CarolRhoda Books, Inc., 1993), p. 24.

3. Marshall W. Fishwick et al., *Illustrious Americans: Jane Addams* (Morristown, N.J.: Silver Burdett Company, 1968), p. 40.

4. Jane Addams, *Twenty Years at Hull-House* (New York: The MacMillan Company, 1910), p. 86.

5. Fishwick et al., p. 39.

6. Ibid., p. 40.

Chapter 6. Finding the Right Place

1. Clara Ingram Judson, *City Neighbor: The Story of Jane Addams* (New York: Charles Scribner's Sons, 1951), p. 55.

2. Ibid., p. 56.

3. Jane Addams, *Twenty Years at Hull-House* (New York: The MacMillan Company, 1910), p. 98.

Chapter 7. Being a Good Neighbor

1. Clara Ingram Judson, *City Neighbor: The Story of Jane Addams* (New York: Charles Scribner's Sons, 1951), p. 68.

2. Marshall W. Fishwick et al., *Illustrious Americans: Jane Addams* (Morristown, N.J.: Silver Burdett Company, 1968), p. 46.

3. Jane Addams, *Twenty Years at Hull-House* (New York: The MacMillan Company, 1910), p. 109.

Chapter 8. Expanding Vision

1. Stephanie Sammartino McPherson, *Peace and Bread: The Story of Jane Addams* (Minneapolis: CarolRhoda Books, Inc., 1993), p. 37.

2. Ibid., p. 38.

3. Jane Addams, *Twenty Years at Hull-House* (New York: The MacMillan Company, 1910), p. 110.

4. McPherson, p. 39.

5. Ibid., p. 40.

6. Clara Ingram Judson, *City Neighbor: The Story of Jane Addams* (New York: Charles Scribner's Sons, 1951), pp. 81–82.

7. McPherson, p. 40.

8. Judson, p. 116.

9. Marshall W. Fishwick et al., *Illustrious Americans: Jane Addams* (Morristown, N.J.: Silver Burdett Company, 1968), p. 54.

Chapter 9. Working for Social Justice

1. Stephanie Sammartino McPherson, *Peace and Bread: The Story of Jane Addams* (Minneapolis: CarolRhoda Books, Inc., 1993), p. 47.

2. Clara Ingram Judson, *City Neighbor: The Story of Jane Addams* (New York: Charles Scribner's Sons, 1951), pp. 119–120.

3. Ibid., p. 119.

4. Cornelia Meigs, *Jane Addams: Pioneer for Social Justice* (New York: Little, Brown & Company, 1970), pp. 95–96.

5. McPherson, p. 52.

6. Ibid.

Chapter 10. Achievements and Legacy

1. Stephanie Sammartino McPherson, *Peace and Bread: The Story of Jane Addams* (Minneapolis: CarolRhoda Books, Inc., 1993), p. 57.

2. Ibid., p. 63.

3. Ibid., p. 65.

4. Cornelia Meigs, *Jane Addams: Pioneer for Social Justice* (New York: Little, Brown & Company, 1970), p. 222.

5. Allen F. Davis, *American Heroine: The Life and Legend of Jane Addams* (New York: Oxford University Press, 1973), p. 244.

6. McPherson, p. 79.

7. Ibid., p. 80.

Chapter 11. Afterword

1. James Weber Linn, *Jane Addams* (New York: D. Appleton-Century Company, 1935), p. 422.

GLOSSARY

anarchism—The theory or doctrine that all forms of government are oppressive and should be abolished.

bookbindery—A place where books are bound.

huckster—A person who sells wares or provisions in the street.

Industrial Revolution—Numerous radical socioeconomic changes that took place in England and America in the late eighteenth and nineteenth centuries as people moved from farms to cities and manufacturing began to replace agriculture as the primary form of commerce.

juvenile court—A court with legal authority over all children under a specified age, usually eighteen.

League of Nations—A world organization established in 1920 to promote international cooperation and peace. Although it was first proposed in 1918 by President Woodrow Wilson, the United States never joined.

philanthropy—The effort to increase the well-being of mankind either through acts of kindness or by financial giving.

Plutarch's Lives—Written by a Greek historian, Plutarch (c. A.D. 46– c. 120), the book compiles forty-six biographies of Greeks and Romans who lived outstanding lives.

Quakers—Nickname for the Society of Friends, a religious group that settled in Pennsylvania.

Victorian England—The period in English history, 1819–1901, when Queen Victoria lived and reigned.

FURTHER READING

Bausum, Ann. *With Courage and Cloth: Winning the Fight for a Woman's Right to Vote*. Washington, D.C.: National Geographic Children's Books, 2004.

Caravantes, Peggy. *Waging Peace: The Story Of Jane Addams*. Greensboro, NC: Morgan Reynolds Publishing, 2004.

Fradin, Dennis Brindell and Judith Bloom Fradin. *Jane Addams: Champion of Democracy*. New York: Clarion Books, 2006.

Greenwood, Janette Thomas. *The Gilded Age: A History in Documents*. New York: Oxford University Press, 2000.

Hopkinson, Deborah. *Shutting Out the Sky: Life in the Tenements of New York, 1880-1924*. New York: Orchard Books, 2003.

Simon, Charnan. *Jane Addams: Pioneer Social Worker*. Danbury, Conn.: Children's Press, 1998.

Slavicek, Louise C. *Jane Addams: Humanitarian*. New York: Chelsea House Publications, 2011.

INDEX